Teacher Take-Out 2
for Preschoolers

12 Complete Lessons for Teachers on the Go!

Created by **M**elinda **M**ahand

ISBN 0805402004

©1997 Broadman & Holman Supplies, Nashville, TN, printed in USA.

Day 1: The Day God Worked in the Dark

Close your eyes and cover them with your hands. What do you see? Is it black and dark?

That's what the whole world was like in the beginning. There was darkness—and there was God.

Then God said, "Let there be light." And there was light! God made the light!

When God saw the light, He liked it. He said the light was good.

Then God separated the light from the darkness. God called the light day. He called the darkness night.

The dark evening and the bright morning made the very first day.

God had worked hard that very first day of creation. In the midst of all the darkness, God had made light.

From Genesis 1:1-5

Bible Song Time
A Song for Darkness and Light
(tune "For He's a Jolly Good Fellow")

When you are scared of the darkness,
When you are scared of the darkness,
When you are scared of the darkness,
Remember God is there.
Remember God is there, Remember God is there,
When you are scared of the darkness,
Remember God is there.

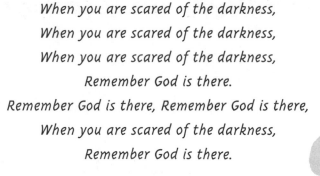

When you have fun in the daytime,
When you have fun in the daytime,
When you have fun in the daytime,
Remember God made light.
Remember God made light, Remember God made light,
When you have fun in the daytime,
Remember God made light.

Day 2: God's Plan for the Sky

Take a deep breath and hold it. Now let it out slowly. What did you just breath in through you nose? That's right. It was air.

When God was making our world, He had a plan. God planned to make people and animals. He planned that the people and animals would breath air. So before God made the people and animals, God needed to make a sky,—a sky full of air for people and animals to breath.

When God was making our world, He had more plans, too. God planned to make birds and butterflies, bees and beetle bugs. He planned for the birds and butterflies, bees and beetle bugs to fly. So before God made birds and butterflies, bees and beetle bugs, God needed to make a sky,—a sky big and wide, with plenty of room for birds and butterflies, bees and beetle bugs to fly.

When God was making our world, He had even more plans. God planned to make a sun and a moon and stars. He planned for the sun, moon, and stars to shine light down onto the earth. So before God made a sun and a moon and stars, God needed to make a sky,—a sky tall and high, with lots of space for the sun, moon, and stars to shine.

That is why, on the second day of creation...
> before God made people and animals,
> before God made birds or butterflies, bees or beetle bugs,
> before God made the sun and moon and stars...

God said, "Let there be a sky!" And there was a sky. God made the sky tall and high, big and wide, and full of air—just the way He had planned.

From Genesis 1:8

Bible Song Time
Soaring Through the Sky
(tune "Mulberry Bush")

This is the way the bluebirds fly, (flap arms like wings)
Bluebirds fly, bluebirds fly,
This is the way the bluebirds fly,
Soaring through the sky.

Also sing:
This is the way the honeybees fly, (place hands on shoulders and flap arms)
....Buzzing through the sky.

This is the way the airplanes fly, (hold arms out straight)
...Zooming through the sky.

This is the way the puffy clouds fly, (grasp hands above head so your arms form a circle)
....Floating through the sky.

Explain: "Clouds in the sky go wherever the wind blows them. In this game, I will be the wind." Ask the other child[ren] to form a row facing you. In order for the game to move quickly, stand only about five large steps away from the child[ren].

Give an instruction such as, "Take one baby step." Before moving, the preschoolers ask, "Strong Wind, may I?" You th[en] answer, "Yes, you may." If a child moves before asking, he goes back to the starting line. Other moves include one gi[ant] step, two hops, one tiptoe, two skating steps, and three hops on one foot.

The game is over when a child reaches you. Play again giving a preschooler an opportunity to be the wind.

Sky Ball

Wad a piece of paper into a ball for each child. Say: "In this game, we try not to let the balls touch the ground. Try [to] keep them up in the sky." Ask: "Can you toss your ball up in the air and catch it?" "Can you toss your ball and catc[h it] twice in a row?" "Can you toss your ball and catch it three times in a row?"

Then alter the game by guiding each child to find a partner. Each pair of children needs only one paper ball. Gu[ide] the children to stand in two rows with partners facing each other. In each pair of children, one partner tosses the ball [to] the other. Then they both take a step backwards and toss the ball again. Continue taking a backwards step and tossi[ng] the ball as far as the children can go.

Bible Craft Time
Make a Sky Painting

What you need:
• paper
• watery blue paint
• straws

1st . . . . Put some watery blue paint on a piece of paper.

2nd . . . Blow through a straw to move the paint around on t[he] paper.

3rd . . . Comment: "You are making a sky painting. The wind blows around in the sky just like the paint is blowing around on your paper."

Day 3: God's Busy Day

Do you remember what God made on the first day of creation when everything was dark? Do you remember what God made on the second day of creation?

On the first day of creation, God made just one thing—light. On the second day of creation, God made just one thing—sky. But on the third day of creation, God made three things.

First, God saw that water covered the whole earth. There was water everywhere! So God spoke to the water. "Roll back! Gather into one place," God said to the water. Then God formed the water into oceans, and God saw that the oceans were good.

When the water rolled back, something new appeared. Dry land appeared where the water had been. God formed the dry land into mountains and valleys, and God saw that the dry land was good.

Then God said, "Let plants grow on the dry land." Suddenly fruit trees and flowers, vegetable plants and green grass appeared all over the land. Inside each plant was something very special. Each plant had its own kind of seed inside so that more plants just like it could grow. The apple tree had apple seed inside the apples. The pumpkin vine had pumpkin seed inside the pumpkins. The rose bush had rose seed inside the roses. God looked at all the beautiful plants He had made, and God saw that they were good.

Then the third day of creation was over. God had made three things—oceans, land, and plants. It had been a very busy day.

From Genesis 1:9-13

Bible Song Time
Creation Day Three
(tune "She'll Be Comin' Round the Mountain")

On day three God made the dry land and the seas, (hold up 3 fingers)
On day three God made the dry land and the seas,
On day three God made the land and seas,
He made them all for you and me, (point to others then self)
On day three God made the dry land and the seas. (hold up 3 fingers)

On day three God made the flowers, plants, and trees, (hold up 3 fingers)
On day three God made the flowers, plants, and trees,
On day three God made flowers, plants, and trees,
He made them all for you and me, (point to others then self)
On day three God made the flowers, plants, and trees. (hold up 3 fingers)

Bible Fun Time
Fruit Basket Turnover

Cut a red circle, a yellow circle, and an orange circle from construction paper. Place the circles on the floor. Remark: "In our Bible story, we learned God made plants that grow fruit. So today let's play fruit basket turnover. Let's pretend the red circle is an apple, the orange circle is an orange, and the yellow circle is a lemon. Listen carefully to hear which piece of fruit to move to." Then give instructions such as:

"If you are wearing something red, hop to the apple."

"If you have a brown eyes, tiptoe to the lemon."

"If you are wearing long pants, walk backwards to the orange."

"If you have a brother, skip to the lemon."

"If you have a dog, hop on one foot to the apple and sit down."

Continue until each child moves several times.

Water Ways

Invite each child to take a turn playing out something you can do with water. A preschooler may need you to suggest something for him to play out, such as swimming, drinking, bathing, washing dishes, washing hair, watering plants, or washing the car. Other girls and boys can guess what the child is playing out.

Bible Craft Time
Watch a Seed Grow

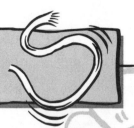

You will need:
- dry lima beans
- large bowl of water
- paper towels
- masking tape
- sandwhich bags which zip-close
- felt-tip marker
- spray bottle of water

1st . . . . Soak the lima beans overnight in a large bowl of water.

2nd . . . Drain off the water.

3rd . . . Guide a child to fold a paper towel and lightly spray it with water. Put the paper towel inside a sandwich bag.

4th . . . Place a lima bean on the paper towel inside the bag.

5th . . . Put a piece of masking tape on the outside of the bag. Print the child's name on the tape.

6th . . . Tell the child to place the bag on a window sill at home. The child will be able to see the bean sprout and begin to grow inside the bag.

Day 4: Why the Sky Isn't Empty Anymore

When you look up in the sky, what do you see? Do you see birds and clouds? Do you see the sun? At night, do you see the moon and stars?

One day God looked at the sky. Do you know what God saw? He saw nothing. There was nothing in the sky. The sky was empty.

So on the fourth day of creation, God said, "Let there be lights in the sky." And God made the sun, the moon, and the stars. He placed them in the sky to shine down on the earth and give it light.

"These lights will help people know when it is daytime and when it is night," said God. "They will help people count the days and the years."

Then God looked at the sun and the moon and the stars. God saw that they were good.

Now still today, the sky is full of bright, warm sunshine during the daytime. At night, the sky is full of glowing moonlight and beautiful, twinkling stars. The sky isn't empty anymore.

From Genesis 1:14-19

Bible Song Time
Shining Time
(tune "Are You Sleeping?")

Lay your head down, Lay your head down, (lay head on hands as if sleeping)
Snuggle tight, Snuggle tight,
Moon and stars are shining, Moon and stars are shining,
Say good night, Say good night.

Stretch and yawn, Stretch and yawn, (stretch and yawn)
Time to play, Time to play,
Now the sun is shining, Now the sun is shining,
Say good day, Say good day.

For added fun, sing a phrase and let the preschoolers echo it back to you.

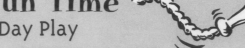

Remark: "It's fun to play on a sunny day. Let's pretend we are outside in the sunshine." Lead the girls and boys in movement.

Pat your head.	Grab your knees.	Nod your head.	Wave to friends.
Reach up high.	Rub your nose.	Turn around.	Wiggle around.
Touch your toes.	Flap your arms.	Clap your hands.	Touch your shoulders.
Now close your eyes.	Now tap your toes.	Now touch the ground.	Now sit back down.

For added fun, repeat one verse faster and faster.

Shooting Star

Cut a long strand of yarn or string. Locate a an item to be the "shooting star" such as a large wooden bead, a large button, a ring, or a thread spool. Slide the shooting star onto the string. Tie the ends of the string together so that it forms a circle. Ask the boys and girls to stand in a circle, grasping the string with both hands. Show them how to slide the shooting star around the string by putting their fists loosely around the string and sliding them back and forth along the string. After they have practiced, encourage them to try to slide the shooting star without letting you see where it is. Say: "Be sure not to hold onto the shooting star. Keep moving it around the circle." As the preschoolers move the shooting star around the string, a teacher or a child stands in the middle of the circle and tries to guess where the shooting star is. The preschoolers moving the shooting star try not to let the person in the middle see where it is.

Bible Craft Time
Make a Sun Catcher

You will need:
- waxed paper
- sandwich bags that zip
- scissors
- iron
- crayons
- extension cord
- vegetable grater
- an old towel

1st . . . . Grate the crayons with a vegetable grater. Place each color of grated crayon in an individual zip-lock bag

2nd . . . Tear off a piece of waxed paper. Invite a child to sprinkle different colors of grated crayon onto the pape

3rd . . . Place a second piece of waxed paper on top of the firs

4th . . . Cover your ironing surface with an old towel. Set you iron on low heat. An adult must be with the iron at a times. Keep the iron out of preschoolers' reach.

5th . . . Put the waxed paper on top of the towel. Carefully iron the paper until the grated crayon melts.

6th . . . When the paper cools, encourage the child to trim it into a circle.

7th . . . The child can tape the sun catcher to a window at hom

Day 5: It's Time Now

Do any of you have a pet fish or a pet bird? Where does the fish swim? Where does the bird fly?

The Bible tells us that in the beginning there weren't any fish. There weren't any birds either. Then God looked at the world He had started making. He saw the oceans and the lakes and the rivers. "It's time now," thought God. "It's time for the fish."

So God said, "Let there be fish swimming in the water." And God made goldfish, jellyfish, and catfish. He made stingrays, starfish, and sharks. God made every kind of fish that swims in the water, and God saw that the fish were good.

Then God looked at His world again. He saw the big blue sky full of warm sunshine. He saw the plants full of seed. "It's time now," thought God. "It's time for the birds."

So God said, "Let there be birds flying in the sky." And God made canaries, parakeets, and cardinals. He made eagles, ducks, and turkeys. God made every kind of bird that flies in the sky, and God saw that the birds were good.

What if God had made fish before He made water? The fish would have died. What if God had made birds before He made a sky for them to fly in or plants for them to eat? The birds would have died. So God waited until the fifth day of creation. He knew that day was just the right time to make the fish and the birds.

From Genesis 1:20-23

Bible Song Time
Did You Know?
(tune "If You're Happy and You Know It")

Did you know that our God made the little birds? (flap arms like wings)
Did you know that our God made the little birds?
You can see them flying high
When you look up in the sky.
Did you know that our God made the little birds?

Did you know that our God made the little fish? (wiggle hand like a fish)
Did you know that our God made the little fish?
They are beautiful to see
As they swim so wild and free.
Did you know that our God made the little fish?

Bible Fun Time
Fish Ball

Cut fish shapes from different colors of construction paper. Tape a fish onto each child's chest. Begin by saying, "I will roll the ball to red fish." Roll the ball to a child who has a red fish. Then give instructions such as: "Red fish roll to blue fish. Blue fish roll to yellow fish. Yellow fish roll to another yellow fish." Make sure each child has a turn to roll the ball.

Beanbag Birds

Locate a laundry basket and several beanbags. If beanbags are not available, stuff zip-lock bags with newspaper instead. Comment: "Today we learned that God made the birds. Let's pretend these beanbags are birds and this laundry basket is their nest. Can you help the bird fly back to its nest?"

Invite each child to try to toss a beanbag into the basket. Ask the children to try tossing with their left hands or tossing with their eyes closed. Encourage them to stand with their backs to the basket and toss over their shoulders or between their legs. Gradually move the basket farther away to increase the challenge.

Bible Craft Time
Make Birdseed Bread

You will need:
- toaster oven or toaster
- paper towels
- bread
- squeeze butter
- plastic knives or craft sticks
- shelled sunflower seed or sesame seed

1st .... Check for food allergies. Place a sign on the door that says: "Today the children will taste bread, butter, and sesame or sunflower seed. Is your child allergic?"

2nd ... Encourage the boys and girls to spread butter onto pieces of bread.

3rd ... Guide the children to carefully sprinkle the seed onto their bread.

4th ... Toast the bread in a toaster oven. (Option: If you do not have a toaster oven, toast the bread in a toaster. Then invite the children to add butter and seed.)

5th ... Say: "Birds eat little seeds like these. The seeds come from plants outside. God made the birds and the plants that feed the birds."

Day 5:
It's Time Now
Activity Sheet

Read the color on the fishing pole.
Use that color to trace the line from the pole to the fish.

Day 5:
It's Time Now
Activity Sheet

Circle the bird that is the same as the first one.

Day 6: Something's Missing

Do you remember what God made to swim in the water? Do you remember what God made to fly in the sky?

On the sixth day of creation, God looked at His world once again. He saw the fish in the water. He saw the birds in the sky. But when God looked at the dry land, He knew there was still something missing. There were no animals to live on the land.

"Let there be animals to live on the dry land," said God. So God made big animals like elephants and lions and horses. He made small animals like mice and spiders and ladybugs. God made furry animals like rabbits and cats and dogs. He made scaly animals like snakes and lizards and turtles. He even made slimy animals like frogs and worms and snails. God made every kind of animal that lives on the dry land, and God saw that the animals were good.

Then God thought: "Something is still missing. My world needs someone to take care of it. There needs to be someone to take care of the fish and the birds and the animals. There needs to be someone to take care of the plants. There needs to be someone to live in my world and enjoy it. Most of all, there needs to be someone I can love."

So God made His most wonderful creation of all. God made people. He made a man, and He made a woman. God showed the people where they could find food, and He told them to take good care of His world.

Then God looked at all the things He had made, and God saw that they were good. Nothing was missing anymore.

From Genesis 1:24-31

Bible Song Time
Can You?
(tune "London Bridge")

Can you wiggle like the snake, (hold hands over head and wiggle)

Like the snake, like the snake,

Can you wiggle like the snake,

That our God made?

Also sing:

Can you hop up like the frog? (crouch on ground and then hop up)

Can you fly like the blue bird? (flap arms like wings)

Can you crawl like the spider? (crawl in place)

Can you stretch like the giraffe? (stretch tall)

Can you sway like elephants? (bend at waist and sway)

Can you march like people? (march in place)

Bible Fun Time
I Know Someone God Made

Explain: "I'm going to describe someone God made. Raise your hand when you think you know the person I'm describing."

Then begin describing someone in the room, such as: "I know someone God made. The person has on a blue shirt. The person has brown hair. The person's name begins with the letter A." When a child raises his hand, ask, "Do you know who God made?" If the child does not name the person you had in mind, continue describing. When a child guesses correctly, describe another preschooler. Continue until you describe each child.

Animal Action

When a child answers a riddle below, let everyone pretend to be the animal. Ask how people can be kind to the animal.

I know an animal that sings a pretty song.
Its feathers are soft, and its wings are strong.
Do you know what it is?

I know an animal that might live at your house.
It likes to climb a tree or catch a mouse.
Do you know what it is?

I know an animal that comes when you call.
It likes to chase a car or fetch a ball.
Do you know what it is?

I know an animal that eats a lot of hay.
It chews and moos all day.
Do you know what it is?

I know an animal that's wooly as can be.
It says "baa, baa" to me.
Do you know what it is?

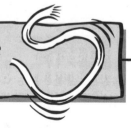

Bible Craft Time
Make a Butterfly

You will need:
- coffee filters
- spray bottle of water
- washable markers
- paper
- clothespins or large paper clips

1st . . . . Set a coffee filter on top of a piece of paper.
2nd . . . Encourage a child to draw on the filter with washable markers.
3rd . . . Lightly spray the filter with water and watch the color run together. Were any new colors created?
4th . . . Allow the filter to dry.
5th . . . Make a butterfly by clipping the filter in the middle with a clothespin or paper clip.
6th . . . Remind the child, "God made butterflies."

Day 6: Something's Missing
Activity Sheet

Draw a line from each animal to its home.

Bird

Horse

Bees

Ants

Bear

Barn

Beehive

Cave

Anthill

Nest

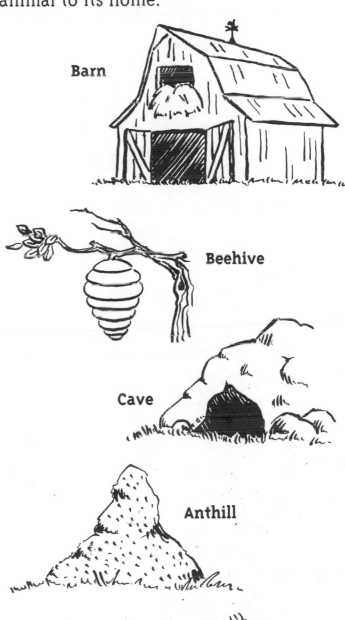

Day 6:
Something's Missing
Activity Sheet

Find and color the snake, grasshopper, frog, and squirrel.

Day 7: The Day God Decided to Rest

Have you ever been really, really tired? What's something you do that makes you tired? Isn't it good to sit down and rest after you work hard or play hard?

The Bible tells us that God worked hard to make the world. Let's count how many days God worked. Each time I say a number, hold up a finger. On the first day (hold up 1 finger), God worked hard to make light. On the second day (hold up 2 fingers), God worked hard to make the sky. On the third day (hold up 3 fingers), God worked hard to make the oceans, the land, and the plants. On the fourth day (hold up 4 fingers), God worked had to make the sun, moon, and stars. On the fifth day (hold up 5 fingers), God worked hard to make fish and birds. And on the sixth day (hold up 6 fingers), God worked hard to make animals and people. So how many days did God work? He worked hard for six days.

When the seventh day came (hold up 7 fingers), God said, "I am finished making the world. Now I will rest." So God did not do any work on the seventh day. He just rested all day long.

From Genesis 2:1-3

Bible Song Time
Creation Song
(tune "Mary Had a Little Lamb")

Children stand in a circle and hold hands. Then walk in a circle as they sing:

In six days God made the world, made the world, made the world,
In six days God made the world, just for you and for me.

Still holding hands, children stop walking and crouch on floor.
On day seven God rested, God rested, God rested,
On day seven God rested, from all of His hard work.

Stand and repeat song.

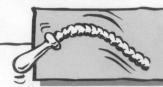 

Bible Fun Time
What Did God Make?

Gather nature items from your area, such as a rock, a leaf, a pinecone, a shell, a twig, a vegetable, a fruit, a nut, or a flower. Place the items in a sack so the children cannot see them.

Ask the boy and girls to sit in a circle. Invite a child sit in front of you with her back to you. Ask the child to place her hands behind her back. Say: "I'm going to put something in your hands. It's something God made. Can you guess what it is without looking at it? Just feel of it, and see if you know what it is."

Place an item in her hand. If she does not guess what it is, give hints such as: "It grows on a tree. You eat it." When the child guesses correctly, give a turn to another preschooler.

God's World

Explain: "I'm going to think of something in this room. See if you can guess what it is." Say, "I see something in God's world, and the color is yellow." Encourage the children to name yellow items in the room until someone guesses the item you had in mind. That person then thinks of an item and says, "I see something in God's world, and the color is (name the color)."

Bible Craft Time
Make a "Resting" Doorknob Sign

You will need:
- paper
- hole punch
- scissors
- yarn
- crayons
- glue

1st.... Guide a child to cut a piece of paper into any shape he chooses.

2nd... Punch two holes in the top of the shape.

3rd... Tie a strand of yarn through the holes so the shape can hang on a doorknob.

4th... Print the word "Resting" on the doorknob sign. (Older preschoolers may be able to copy the word onto their doorknob signs.)

5th... Invite the child to decorate the sign with crayons, scraps of yarn, and scraps of paper.

6th... Comment: "Hang this sign on your doorknob when you are resting. The sign reminds people to be quiet. Maybe someone else in your family would like to use the sign, too." Add: "Everybody needs rest. God worked hard for six days to create our world. Do you remember what He did on the seventh day?"

Day 7: The Day God Decided to Rest

Activity Sheet

Help Betty butterfly match the blossom to the flower.
Cut out the blossoms.
Glue them on the matching flower.
Color Betty and the flowers.

Day 7: The Day God Decided to Rest

Activity Sheet

Write 1 or • to show what God made first.
Write 2 or •• to show what God made second.
Write 3 or ••• to show what God made third.
Write 4 or •••• to show what God made fourth.
Write 5 or ••••• to show what God made fifth.
Write 6 or •••••• to show what God made sixth.

The King Who Loved to Count

I wonder how many people are here today. Let's count around the circle and find out. (Count each teacher and child out loud.) Sometimes it's fun to count people and see how many there are.

Long ago there lived a mighty king named Caesar Augustus. One day Caesar Augustus decided he wanted to count all the people in his land.

"I want each person to be counted," said Caesar Augustus. "Leave no one out. Each person must travel to the city his family is from. Then each person will be counted."

When Joseph and Mary heard the news, they knew they must be counted, too.

"My family is from Bethlehem," said Joseph. "So we must go to Bethlehem to be counted."

The trip to Bethlehem was a long one. Mary and Joseph did not have a car like we do today. They had to walk or ride a donkey. It took Joseph and Mary a long time to walk to Bethlehem, but finally they arrived.

"Here we are," said Joseph. "Now we can be counted, too."

From Luke 2:1-5

Bible Song Time
Going to Bethlehem
(tune "London Bridge")

We will walk to Bethlehem, Bethlehem, Bethlehem, (walk in place)
We will walk to Bethlehem, and be counted.

We will ride* to Bethlehem, Bethlehem, Bethlehem, (pretend to ride a donkey)
We will ride to Bethlehem, and be counted.

*Suggest other ways Mary and Joseph might have traveled to Bethlehem, such as "march," "run," or "hop." Sing about each way as you move in place.

Bible Fun Time
Traveling Game

Locate a small, lightweight suitcase or tote bag. Ask the girls and boys to stand in a circle. As you play music on a record player or cassette tape recorder, the children can begin passing the suitcase around the circle. When you stop the music, look to see who is holding the suitcase. That child gets to "travel" to a new place in the circle. Then he begins passing the suitcase again as you start the music.

Counting Action

Locate a beanbag or a plastic snap-on lid such as from a margarine tub. Place five pieces of paper on the floor. On each paper, print the numeral 1, 2, 3, 4, or 5. Invite a child to toss the beanbag or lid and see which numeral it lands on. The child then names an action for everyone to do that number of times. Possible actions include: turn around, touch your toes, hop, bend your knees, nod your head, or clap your hands. For example, if a child tosses the beanbag onto the numeral 2 and then says, "Clap your hands," everyone would clap their hands two times. Let each child have a turn to toss the beanbag or lid.

Bible Craft Time
Make a Road Map Painting

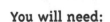

You will need:
- toy cars
- liquid tempera paint or washable felt-tip markers
- paper
- an aluminum pie pan or a roll of masking tape

1st. . . . Pour liquid tempera paint into an aluminum pie pan until you have just covered the bottom of the pan. If tempera paint is not available, tape a felt-tip marker onto the front of each toy car.

2nd. . . Invite a child to dip the wheels of a car in the paint and roll the car along on the paper. The wheels will leave a track print. If you are using markers instead, the marker will leave a print as the child rolls the car.

3rd. . . Remark: "Sometimes a family travels in a car. When Joseph and Mary traveled to Jerusalem, they did not have a car. Do you remember how they traveled?"

The King Who Loved to Count

Activity Sheet

Help Mary and Joseph travel to Bethlehem.

The King Who Loved to Count

Activity Sheet

Connect the dots to discover how many people travel today.

The World's Strangest Motel

When you travel with your family, where do you spend the night? Do you stay at Grandma's house? Do you stay in a motel? Have you ever gone on a trip and spent the night in a barn?

When Joseph and Mary traveled to Bethlehem, they needed a place to spend the night. But when they came to the inn, which was like a motel, there weren't any rooms left. Where could Joseph and Mary spend the night?

Finally Joseph took Mary to a stable. A stable is a place where animals stay, like a barn. Can you imagine spending the night in a barn full of animals? Well, that's exactly where Joseph and Mary spent the night.

Mary was happy to have a place to stay. She laid down on the hay to rest. That night something very special happened in the stable. Baby Jesus was born!

Mary rocked Baby Jesus in her arms. She wrapped soft cloths around Him to keep Him warm. Then Mary laid Baby Jesus in a manger to sleep.

Yes, the stable made a strange motel, but Baby Jesus made it a special night.

From Luke 2:6-7

Bible Song Time
Mary Loved Jesus
(tune "Jesus Loves Me" chorus)

Mary loved Jesus, (pretend to rock a baby in your arms)
Mary loved Jesus,
Mary loved Jesus,
She took good care of Him.

She wrapped Him in cloths, (circle one arm around the other)
She wrapped Him in cloths,
She wrapped Him in cloths,
To keep Him safe and warm.

She laid Him in bed, (lay head on hands as if sleeping)
She laid Him in bed,
She laid Him in bed,
A manger full of hay.

Bible Fun Time
Memory Game

Gather a towel and four baby items, such as a pacifier, a baby spoon, a bottle, and a bib.

Sit in a circle on the floor. Lay the items in front of you. Point to each item and say what it is. Then cover the items with the towel.

Ask the boys and girls to close their eyes as you reach beneath the towel and remove an item. When the item is behind your back, say, "Open your eyes!" Lift the towel and see if the children can name the missing item. Replace the item and begin again.

Room at the Inn

Get a chair for all the children but two. Place the chairs back to back in a row. Remark: "Each chair is a room at the inn. Walk around the chairs while the music plays. When the music stops, get a room at the inn by sitting in a chair. The two people who do not get a room are Mary and Joseph."

Play a record or cassette tape of Christmas music as the girls and boys walk around the chairs. Stop the music and remind the children to sit down. The two children who do not get a chair are "Mary and Joseph." Mention who they are, but do not take them out of the game. Simply start the music to play the game again and find a new "Mary and Joseph."

Bible Craft Time
Make Christmas Ornaments

You will need:
- sandpaper
- scissors
- ribbon or yarn
- cinnamon sticks
- crayons (glitter crayons work especially well)
- hole punch

1st . . . . Cut out star, gingerbread boy, and candy cane sha[pes] from sandpaper. (Tip: If you have cookie cutters in these shapes, trace around the cookie cutters onto [the] sandpaper and cut out the shapes. Older preschool[ers] can do this step.)

2nd . . . Punch a hole in the top of each shape. Tie a loop of ribbon or yarn through the hole.

3rd . . . Encourage a child to rub a sandpaper ornament wi[th] a cinnamon stick. The cinnamon adds a pleasant aroma and a dark brown color to the sandpaper.

4th . . . Invite the child to color on the ornament with crayo[ns.]

5th . . . When a child chooses a gingerbread boy shape, remind the child: "Jesus was a baby boy. He was b[orn] in Bethlehem." When a child chooses a candy cane shape, comment: "This ornament looks like a shep-herd's staff. Shepherds came to visit Baby Jesus." When a child chooses a star shape, say: "After Jesu[s] was born, wise men came to visit Him. The wise me[n] followed a star to the place where Jesus lived."

The World's Strangest Motel
Activity Sheet

Draw a line from the baby to each thing a baby would use.
Draw a line form the child to each thing an older child would use.

Baby

Older Child

Fork

Bike

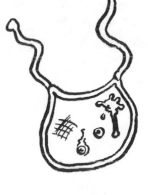

Bib

Bottle

Cup

Rattle

The World's Strangest Motel

Activity Sheet

Color the manger scene.
You may also choose to draw sheep and a donkey.

A Night of Unusual Sights

What do you see when you go outside at night?

The Bible tells about some shepherds who saw something very unusual one night. The shepherds were outside in a field. All around them, lying in the grass, the shepherds saw their sheep. But that was not unusual. The shepherds saw their sheep lying in the grass every night.

Shining up in the sky, the shepherds saw the moon and stars. But that was not unusual either. The shepherds saw the moon and stars shining in the sky every night.

All of a sudden, standing right in front of them, the shepherds saw an angel. That was very unusual. The shepherds had never seen an angel before. They were very frightened.

"Do not be afraid," said the angel. "I have good news for you. Baby Jesus has been born in Bethlehem. You will find Him wrapped in cloths and lying in a manger."

Suddenly many more angels appeared to the shepherds. The angels praised God and then went away into heaven.

When the angels were gone, the shepherds said, "Let's go to Bethlehem. Let's go see Baby Jesus."

So the shepherds hurried to Bethlehem. There they found Mary and Joseph. They found Baby Jesus lying in the manger. "Thank You, God," said the shepherds. "Thank you for letting us see Jesus."

From Luke 2:8-20

Bible Song Time
Shepherd's Song
(tune "Mulberry Bush")

The angels sang to the shepherds, (Clasp your hands above your head to form a circle)
To the shepherds, to the shepherds,
The angels sang to the shepherds,
They sang of Baby Jesus.

The shepherds went to Bethlehem, (walk in place)
To Bethlehem, to Bethlehem,
The shepherds went to Bethlehem,
To find the Baby Jesus.

In Bethlehem they found Jesus, (pretend to rock a baby in your arms)
They found Jesus, they found Jesus,
In Bethlehem they found Jesus,
A-lying in a manger.

"We thank You, God," the shepherds sang, (fold hands as if in prayer)
The shepherds sang, the shepherds sang,
"We thank You, God," the shepherds sang,
When they saw Baby Jesus.

Bible Fun Time
Guess Who?

Encourage a child pretend to be something from today's Bible story. If a child needs help thinking of character to pretend to be, suggest a shepherd, an angel, a sheep, Mary, Joseph, or Baby Jesus. As the preschooler pretends, the other girls and boys can guess who the Bible character is.

What Do You Hear?

Say: "The shepherds heard a special sound on the night Jesus was born. The shepherds heard angels singing. Now let's see what sounds you can hear in our room today."

Ask the boys and girls to close their eyes. Make a sound by clapping your hands, snapping your fingers, clicking your tongue, whistling, or tapping your foot on the floor. Ask the preschoolers to identify the sound. Then let the children make the same sound. Play again using another of the sounds.

Bible Craft Time
Make Shepherd's Staff Candy

You will need:
- small candy canes
- electric skillet
- a cookie sheet or cake pan
- spatula
- a rolling pin or small hammer
- white almond bark
- sandwich bags that zip close
- a hot mitt

1st.... Check for food allergies. Place a sign on the door tha says: "Today the children will taste candy made from white almond bark and candy canes. Is your child allergic?"

2nd... Place unwrapped candy canes in a sandwich bag. Crush the candy canes with the hammer or rolling pi Tell the boys and girls: "These candy canes are shap like shepherds' staffs. The shepherds came to visit Baby Jesus in Bethlehem."

3rd... Melt white almond bark in an electric skillet set on degrees. Remind the children not to touch the hot skillet. Supervise carefully.

4th... Guide a child to wear the hot mitt and stir the melti almond bark with the spatula.

5th... Pour crushed candy canes into the melted almond bark and stir.

6th... Spread the melted candy in a thin layer onto the cool sheet or cake pan. The candy will harden as it cools.

7th... When completely cool, break apart the candy into small pieces. Place some candy in a sandwich bag f each child.

A Night of Unusual Sights

Activity Sheet

Bible Story Review—Circle the correct picture.

What animals were the
shepherds watching?

Who told the shepherds
about Baby Jesus?

Where did the
shepherds go?

How did the shepherds
feel when they saw Jesus?

A Night of Unusual Sights

Activity Sheet

Circle each item on the right that belongs with the shepherds.

The Coat That Meant I Love You

What is your favorite color? (Let each child name a color.) If we put all those colors together in a coat, imagine how beautiful it would be.

Long ago, in a land called Canaan, there lived a boy who had just such a coat. The boy's name was Joseph, and he was seventeen years old. Joseph lived in a big family. He had eleven brothers.

Each day Joseph and his eleven brothers went out in the fields to work for their father. Their job was to take care of their father's sheep. Joseph and his brothers found grass for the sheep to eat. They found water for the sheep to drink. They even protected the sheep from wild animals.

One day Joseph's father walked up to him. "I love you, Joseph," said Joseph's father. "I love you so much that I made this new coat for you."

Joseph's father handed him the new coat. Many different colors were woven into the coat. Joseph's father probably made it out of wool from the sheep Joseph cared for. It was a beautiful coat.

Joseph happily put on the coat. "Thank you, Father," he said. "Each time I put on this coat, I will remember that you love me."

From Genesis 37:1-4

Bible Song Time
The Coat of Many Colors
(tune "Mary Had a Little Lamb")

Give each child a piece of red, yellow, green, or blue paper. Sing the first stanza as the children pass the papers around the circle. When you get to the second stanza, have the children stop passing the papers. As you sing a color, each child with that color of paper can hold the paper up in the air. Sing the second stanza again, putting the colors in a different order.

Joseph had a brand new coat, brand new coat, brand new coat,
Joseph had a brand new coat, his father made for him.

Red and yellow, green and blue, green and blue, green and blue,
Red and yellow, green and blue were colors in his coat.

Bible Fun Time
Color Walk

Select several colors of paper. Cut out a different shape from each color of paper. Cut each shape into two or three pieces. Mix up all the pieces. Then give one to each child.

Ask the girls and boys to walk around the room and look for children with the same color of paper. When the preschoolers with the same color of paper find each other, they come back and sit with the teacher. After all the matches have been found, guide each set of children to put their pieces together and name their shape and color.

Color Toss

Gather several colors of construction paper. Also locate a beanbag or a plastic snap-on lid (such as from a margarine tub). Spread the paper on the floor. Stand in a circle around the paper. Invite a child to toss the beanbag or lid onto one of the colors. Give directions for the preschoolers wearing that color. For example, say: "Everyone wearing blue, touch your toes." "Everyone wearing yellow, hop on one foot." Continue passing the beanbag or lid around the circle until each child has a turn to toss it.

Bible Craft Time
Make a Coat of Many Colors

You will need:
- large paper grocery sacks
- scissors
- crayons or washable felt-tip markers
- construction paper
- paste or glue

1st . . . . Cut a slit up the center of one side of each sack.

2nd . . . Cut arm holes and a neck hole in each sack. If there i printing on the outside of the sack, turn the sack inside out.

3rd . . . Invite a child to cut construction paper designs and glue them on the sack. Use crayons or markers to add the finishing touches.

4th . . . Print the child's name on the inside of the sack.

The Coat That Meant I Love You

Activity Sheet

Draw a line from each person to the coat the person needs.

The Coat That Meant I Love You

Activity Sheet

Color Joseph's Coat

Who Is That Boy?

Do you have a good friend? How did you meet your friend? The Bible tells about two good friends and how they met.

Jonathan was the son of a king. Sometimes Jonathan stayed in the room and listened when his father, the king, talked to important people. One day Jonathan was standing in the room with his father when another boy walked in. Everyone was so excited about this boy!

"Who is that boy and why is everyone making such a fuss?" wondered Jonathan.

Then Jonathan heard his father talk to the boy. This boy had killed a giant named Goliath.

"Who are you, boy?" asked the king.

"My name is David," answered the boy.

Jonathan listened to David talk. "I like him," thought Jonathan. "We could be friends."

Jonathan wanted to give David something to show that they were friends. So Jonathan took off his robe and gave it to David. Then Jonathan took off his armor and his sword. He gave the armor and the sword to David, too.

"I will always be your friend," promised Jonathan.

"I will always be your friend, too," promised David.

From 1 Samuel 18:1-4, 20:42

Bible Song Time
Good Friends
(tune "She'll Be Comin' Round the Mountain")

We can all clap hands with our good friends at church.
We can all clap hands with our good friends at church.
We can all clap hands with our good friends.
We can all clap hands with our good friends.
We can all clap hands with our good friends at church.

Other motions include tap toes, shake hands, reach high, bend low, and nod heads.

Bible Fun Time
Choosing Friends

Ask the preschoolers to sit in a circle on the floor. Invite a child to walk around the outside of the circle. To the tune "Mary Had a Little Lamb," sing: "Morgan came to church today, church today, church today. Morgan came to church today, Now she can choose a friend." When Morgan touches a friend, the friend stands up and walks around the circle as you sing. Play until each child has a turn to walk around the circle and choose a friend.

Friendly Moves

Ask the children to stand facing each other in two rows on opposite sides of the room. Begin the game by choosing a child and telling him to hop to a friend. The child then hops across the room and touches a friend standing in that row. Ask the child he touches to walk backwards to a friend. That child walks backwards across the room and touches a friend in that row. Make sure each child has a turn to move across the room. Other movements include: hop on one foot to a friend

skip to a friend

run to a friend

skate to a friend

crawl backwards to a friend

march to a friend.

Bible Craft Time
Make Friendship Bracelets

You will need:
- plastic rings from soft drink six-packs
- glue
- several colors of dry or liquid tempera paint
- small paintbrushes such as used with watercolors
- aluminum pie pans
- scissors
- paper
- crayon

1st . . . . Pour glue into aluminum pie pans.

2nd . . . Add a small amount of paint to each pan and stir. Offer several colors of glue.

3rd . . . Cut apart each six-pack ring into six individual rings

4th . . . Invite a child to make several friendship bracelets by painting plastic rings with the colorful glue.

5th . . . Print the child's name on a piece of paper. Lay the child's bracelets on the paper to dry.

6th . . . If the bracelets dry in time, encourage the girls and boys to exchange bracelets with their friends.